FIRST IMPRESSIONS

3/00

FIRST IMPRESSIONS

J.M.W. Turner

ROBERT KENNER

Harry N. Abrams, Inc., Publishers

To Sue for affection and correction
To Mom and Dad for inspiration and information
To Bonnie and Clyde for helping

Series Editor: Robert Morton
Editor: Lory Frankel
Designer: Joan Lockhart
Photo Research: Neil Ryder Hoos

Library of Congress Cataloging-in-Publication Data

Kenner, Robert.
J. M.W. Turner / Robert Kenner.
p.   cm.—(First impressions)
Includes bibliographical references and index.
Summary: Discusses the life and work of one of England's greatest
painters, whose work forshadowed that of the Impressionists.
ISBN 0–8109–3868–5 (hardcover)
1. Turner., J. M.W. (Joseph Mallord William), 1775–1851—Juvenile
literature.   2. Painters—England—Biography—Juvenile.
[1. Turner, J. M.W. (Joseph Mallord William), 1775–1851.
2. Artists.   3. Painting, English.]   I. Title.   II Series: First
impressions (New York, N.Y.)
ND497.T8K46   1995
759.2—dc20
[B]   95–7396

Chapter One

"Suppose you look"

No artist ever painted more remarkable sunrises and sunsets than J. M. W. Turner. He found rays of light passing through mist and vapor endlessly fascinating, and he was drawn to the formidable challenge of trying to capture the grandeur of the heavens by placing colors on a flat surface. A Turner sun might be a ghostly glow over dewdrops, a fiery red coal sinking into the ocean, or a blinding white burst of energy that threatens to atomize everything in sight. Turner never ran out of ways to paint the sun in the sky, and he never painted two skies exactly alike.

In order to study the clouds, Turner explained to a friend, he would take a boat, anchor it in a stream, and lie on his back, "gazing at the heavens for

When Turner painted this self portrait, in 1789, he was barely fourteen years old, and hadn't quite mastered his craft, as shown by the clumsily painted hand. He had, however, been admitted to classes at the Royal Academy.

hours, and even days, till he grasped some effect of the light which he desired to transpose to the canvas." While floating around in a little boat may sound leisurely, for Turner it was hard work. From a very early age, his dedication to

As an old man Turner continued reworking his pictures even after they had been hung on gallery walls. He became famous for masterly last minute touch-ups at the Royal Academy's "varnishing days" before exhibitions opened.

art was absolute. Always hungry for visual experience, he got up early enough to watch the sun rise each morning until his death at age seventy-six.

Art was no hobby for Turner: it was his passion, his calling, his life's work. During the time he served as a lecturer at England's Royal Academy of Art, he made this no-nonsense attitude very clear to his students. The short, pudgy, middle-aged man in professorial robes addressed his class with halting speech and a slight cockney accent, but no one could mistake the seriousness of his words. Like a general rallying his troops before battle, Turner described the artistic enterprise as a noble struggle that was of importance to the entire British Empire. Making art was for him a difficult, risky, and heroic activity. Turner held that the artist's solemn responsibility was to equal and outdo his forerunners, to "advance" the profession at any cost. There's no telling whether any of the students in his classroom were equal to the task Turner handed them. But no one worked harder at it than Turner himself.

Turner was a much better artist than he was a teacher. Unlike most other professional painters in England during that time, he almost never took private pupils. Though he became one of the most productive artists in history, few people ever saw him paint or draw. He preferred it that way, not wanting to give away his secret materials, methods, and techniques. One might say he was too busy teaching himself to have time for explaining what other people should do. After he was elected a full member of the Royal Academy, teaching was expected of him, but he lectured as seldom as possible.

"He was often at a loss to find words to express the ideas he wished to communicate," wrote one witness of Turner's lectures. "To aid his memory, he would now and then copy out passages, which, when referred to, he could not clearly read." We know from the amount of preparation and study that Turner invested in these lectures that he wanted to teach well. He took classes almost too seriously, producing elaborate drawings and diagrams to illustrate his complicated ideas about light and shadows. Like many thoughtful people, Turner had difficulty making his big ideas understood. "But when the spirit did stir within him," wrote that same witness after Turner's death, "and he could find utterance to his thoughts, he soared as high above the common order of lecturers as he did in the regions of Art."

For the average student, Turner must have been an intimidating master. While reviewing his pupils' work, if he said anything, it was usually a disapproving grunt. More often, he would attack a student's error with a crayon, slashing across the flawed canvas to correct the composition. If anyone was foolish enough to ask him *how* something should be done, his usual reply was, "Suppose you *look.*"

Turner himself was always looking at things, as much for new ways to communicate what he saw as for the way it made him feel. Art came naturally to him, and it always played an important role in his life. To look, to see, to think, to feel, to know one's place in a tumultuous universe—all of these were linked together for Turner. The term genius has been so misused and overused that it has now lost some of its meaning, but there seems no better way to describe this boy from London who made up his mind to become England's greatest painter, and succeeded.

Turner exhibited this painting along with a quote about the end of the world from the Book of Revelations: "I saw an angel standing in the sun, and he cried with a loud voice, saying to all the fowls that fly in the midst of heaven, Come gather yourselves together unto the supper of the great God, that ye may eat the flesh of kings, the flesh of captains, and the flesh of mighty men."

Chapter Two
His First Strokes

JOSEPH MALLORD WILLIAM TURNER WAS BORN IN LONDON IN 1775. He liked to claim that his birthday was April 23, which happens to be both Shakespeare's birthday and Saint George's Day, a holiday in honor of the patron saint of England. Turner's birth records were lost, leaving him free to invent the details of his beginnings. In spite of—perhaps because of—his humble origins, Turner was always concerned with cultivating a respectable public image. He certainly couldn't have chosen a more auspicious day to be born, suggesting a lad full of both ambition and patriotic spirit.

His father, William Turner, was a short, jovial man who made a comfortable living as a barber and wig maker in the lively London neighborhood

of Covent Garden. Father and son were always very close. Besides teaching his son to read, the elder Turner nurtured the boy's interest in drawing. In those days, children were not required to go to school, which was generally a privilege reserved for wealthy aristocrats. Turner was fortunate to have been guided in life by parents who recognized his creative gift and nurtured it.

From the time the boy was ten, his father liked to boast to clients, "My son, sir, is going to be a painter." Turner's father promoted his son's young career by hanging his drawings in the windows of the barber shop, which was situated

(Previous page) Turner was pleased enough with this pencil sketch to include his own initials and birthdate, carved into a stone slab in the foreground.

This is the room in which Turner was born and lived for many years as a boy. The picture was painted the year after he died by James Wykeham Archer.

above a popular neighborhood tavern. By selling these works for a shilling or two, Turner's father demonstrated that one could make a living from art, provided one lived frugally and stuck to basic principles of business. ("Dad never praised me for anything but saving a half-penny," Turner once recalled.) The artist continued to live and work at his father's home on Maiden Lane until he turned twenty-four, by which time he was nearly successful enough to open his own private gallery. Even then, his father stayed with him to serve as studio assistant, housekeeper, and business advisor. They remained almost inseparable.

One of the earliest accounts of young William, as his father called him, has the boy leaving London at age ten to visit his uncle, a butcher in the small town of Brentford near the Thames River. His younger sister had died, and Turner's parents must have thought a change of scenery would do him good. Being a city boy, he was thrilled by his first contact with England's natural beauty. He didn't have many playmates, but he enjoyed walking along the banks of the river. Turner also attended a small free school while in Brentford. On the way to class, he amused himself by drawing chickens on the stone walls in chalk. He was reportedly a bit of a loner and did not make conversation easily, but he loved to read all sorts of books, from the Bible to translations of Greek mythology and romantic British poetry. Turner's interest in literature remained strong his whole life, and his readings influenced the subjects of his art and the ideas that lay behind his painting.

With all its sights and sounds, Covent Garden must have been a wonderfully stimulating place for a young boy with artistic leanings to grow up. The bustling shopping district, home to London's biggest fruit and flower market, today still buzzes with activity. Turner lived close to the Thames River, where he could gaze at great sailing ships passing by, or the Houses of Parliament, or the majestic dome of Saint Paul's cathedral. The sights and experiences of his boyhood were never far from his mind, and he returned to these same subjects again and again throughout his career.

Turner's neighborhood was also filled with artists, and rather than attending a conventional school, Turner began studying with various masters at the age of eleven. At first, it seemed he might become an architect. He took an interest in perspective, reading books and attending lectures on the subject. Next, he began working in the office of the architect Thomas Hardwick, who recognized Turner's talent and was the first to suggest that he enroll in the Royal Academy.

The Royal Academy of Art was founded in 1768, seven years before Turner's birth, by Sir Joshua Reynolds, an accomplished English painter of portraits and historical scenes who envied the prestigious art academies of Rome and Paris. British painting was not widely admired before Reynolds established what was commonly referred to as the R.A., through which he dearly hoped to begin an "English school" of painting.

The R.A. was not only a place of study and connoisseurship but also a thriving marketplace. To be a successful artist in Turner's day, you had to be a member of the Academy. Turner joined at age fourteen, and over the next sixty-two years, the R.A. became a sort of second family for him. While he experienced many rivalries and disagreements there, his loyalty to the Royal Academy remained strong throughout his life.

Turner was only twelve when he made his first signed and dated watercolor, a copy of an engraving of an old tower near Oxford. The theme of historic buildings set in landscapes would continue to fascinate him throughout his life. At the age of fourteen, he was off to visit his uncle again, this time further away at Sunningwell, near Oxford, where he made his own sketchbook and filled it with his first drawings from nature. Turner reworked some of these sketches of buildings around town, turning them into finished watercolors. The artist hung onto this sketchbook, like all his sketchbooks, for the rest of his life.

Even Turner's early architectural drawings conveyed a certain mood.

When Turner turned fifteen, one of his drawings was shown at the Royal Academy, making him one of the youngest exhibited artists in the history of the institution. *The Archbishop's Palace, Lambeth* was a skillful but comparatively unimaginative drawing for Turner. At the time, his vision was still shaped by his architectural training, and his main goal seems to have been the precise description of the building. Sometime during the spring of 1791, Turner and his artistic vision underwent an important change.

While touring the western countryside, near the Thames again, he began filling his second known sketchbook with more dramatic scenery: a ruined church, a deep river gorge. Instead of making impersonal drawings of buildings, he concentrated on the landscape itself, trying to capture in his work the feelings it

17

While touring the Welsh countryside in 1792, Turner visited the ruins of a medieval monastery, known as Tintern Abbey.

aroused in him. Over time, his drawings became progressively more evocative of a spirit that historians now call romanticism.

The precise meaning of romanticism is not easy to pin down. Less a specific style than a general attitude of thinking, romanticism involved a rejection of established values and a celebration of the individual's thoughts and feelings. In this respect, painters, designers, romantic poets, and musicians helped to bring about new ways of looking at the world, which remain meaningful to this day. They sometimes turned to bygone civilizations for inspiration, especially to ancient Greece, and this particular strain of romanticism became a dominant style known as neoclassicism.

For a true romantic, though, there could be no hard-and-fast rules: the individual was everything; the power of the imagination was surpassed only by that of nature. Travel, danger, social and political upheaval, cataclysmic natural phenomena—these were the stuff of art and life. Turner experienced and even enjoyed all these things, and they informed much of his work, but the word "romantic" cannot fully describe him as it can other, more limited artists. No single label or school could ever contain Turner; he tried every style, mastered them all, then created his own.

But romantic he was, at least in 1792, the year Turner set off on a solitary walking tour of the picturesque Wye River valley in Wales. It was a great time to be a young artist. Music, poetry, and painting were flourishing throughout Europe. The French Revolution had begun, fostering an overwhelming spirit of youthful idealism tinged with just enough terror to keep it exciting. With monarchs losing their heads and democracy on the rise, anything seemed possible. All the old rules were invalid, and art seemed like a good way to heal one's soul, if not the world.

During his tour of the Wye valley, Turner sketched the ivy-covered ruins of

Turner, who enjoyed inside jokes, painted his favorite horse into this cold country landscape and modeled the peasant girl after his own daughter.

an old, abandoned church known as Tintern Abbey. Its crumbling stone walls speak silently of time, nature, and the frailty of man. A few years later, the great romantic poet William Wordsworth would immortalize the same place in a poem published in his famous book of verse called *Lyrical Ballads.* Wordsworth's poem, "Lines Composed a Few Miles Above Tintern Abbey," is as good an explanation of the romantic spirit as any, and Turner's water-color, *Interior of Tintern Abbey,* which he exhibited at the R.A. in 1794, might have served as an illustration for the poem, so closely does it mirror the somber mood of the lines:

One the first oil paintings Turner ever exhibited was this scene of fishermen on a dangerous sea. Ocean adventures fascinated the artist throughout his life.

. . . I have felt

A presence that disturbs me with the joy

Of elevated thoughts; a sense sublime

Of something far more deeply interfused,

Whose dwelling is the light of setting suns,

And the round ocean and the living air,

And the blue sky, and the mind of man. . . .

While Wordsworth claimed that good poetry should be "the spontaneous overflow of powerful feelings," Turner knew that capturing powerful feelings in a picture was hard work, and he never pretended otherwise. One of his many notebooks contains the phrase, "Every look at nature is a refinement upon art." This seems to sum up Turner's relationship to romanticism perfectly.

Turner was soon accepted by the Royal Academy's life drawing class. But since the academy did not offer courses in landscape painting, which Turner preferred, from about 1794, he took part in an informal "academy" operated just a few minutes away from his house by a curious character named Dr. Monro. A specialist in mental illness who lived in splendid rooms overlooking the Thames, the doctor would invite young artists to be his guests for the evening and ask them to make copies of original paintings in exchange for a small fee and supper. Two of his fledgling copyists, Turner and Thomas Girtin, developed into distinguished artists in their own right.

Dr. Monro introduced Turner and Girtin to the work of John Robert Cozens. In 1794, the little-known painter of haunting, moody landscapes had been sent to the Hospital of St. Mary at Bethlehem (also known as "Bedlam"), a London "lunatic asylum," where Dr. Monro cared for the disturbed artist. Today, Cozens is considered a pioneer of romantic landscape painting. Girtin used to trace the outlines of his pictures, and then Turner would fill in the details. Both young artists were deeply affected by their prolonged exposure to Cozens's beautiful yet slightly spooky vision of the English landscape.

At age twenty-one, Turner exhibited his first oil painting. *Fishermen at Sea* (1796) was a bold work that confirmed what Turner's watercolors had only hinted—that this young artist was also a gifted storyteller. He could combine technical skill with a vivid imagination to produce a sense of awe bordering on dread known as "the sublime." The menacing, lead-colored swell of seawater that threatens to swamp the overloaded fishing boat in Turner's painting is eerily lit by the moon, which struggles through the clouds, just as the men in the boat struggle to escape the darkness that surrounds them. In the foreground, seagulls skirt the tops of the waves, oblivious to the plight of the endangered mariners. So powerful is this scene of humans at the mercy of nature in one of its violent moods that one can easily overlook how technically challenging the painting was.

In this self-portrait of 1798 the young artist has toned down his flamboyant attire and appears to be taking himself more seriously.

In *Fishermen at Sea,* Turner successfully rendered three different kinds of light in oil paint—moonlight through clouds, moonlight reflected off a stormy sea, and the glow of the ship's lantern. To attempt such a challenging task in one's

Turner studied the works of past masters carefully and often tried to outpaint artists he admired. This pretty portrait reflects his admiration of Rembrandt.

first oil painting was ambitious; to exhibit the work at the Academy was down-right courageous. Turner was quickly mastering all the possibilities of his new medium; his future as an "artist of consequence" seemed assured.

Turner sold his first oil for ten pounds—a substantial sum equivalent to several months' wages—and began to receive favorable notices in the press. That same year he competed for an associate membership in the Academy but lost the election. Having "more commissions than he could execute," as he told a colleague at the time, must have helped ease his disappointment. Another comfort was the affection of Sarah Danby, a young actress and singer married to John Danby, a songwriter Turner knew and admired. Soon after Danby died, Sarah became Turner's mistress. Evalina, the first of his three children by Sarah, was born in 1799. Turner supported Sarah and the family, but the couple never married. He was so reluctant to make any commitment that might interfere with his art and his travels that he never even moved in with her.

Just as the eighteenth century was coming to a close, Turner's artistic horizons expanded considerably. In May 1799, the wealthy collector William Beckford, who had recently become a patron of Turner, returned from Italy with two paintings by the renowned French landscape artist Claude Lorrain. Turner had admired Claude's delicate handling of light in engraved reproductions (there was no color printing then) but had never traveled to the European continent to see the real thing. When Beckford invited a number of artists to view the paintings at his home, it was Turner's first opportunity to see the old master's work in person. A fellow artist who witnessed Turner's first glimpse of Claude's *Sacrifice to Apollo* reported that Turner was "both pleased and unhappy while he viewed it—it seemed to be beyond his power of imitation." Claude continued to have a powerful effect on Turner and his work for some time. Years later, when he first saw Claude's *Seaport with the Embarkation of Saint Ursula,* he reportedly burst into tears.

Even after he'd traveled the globe and secured his own place as one of the world's most celebrated living painters, Turner always experienced a mixture of envy and esteem whenever he saw such magnificent work by another artist. "Study therefore the great works of the great masters," Sir Joshua Reynolds had written, "consider them as models which you are to imitate, and at the same time as rivals with whom you are to contend." Turner took the advice a step further to include his successful contemporaries. Apparently, he often adopted the subject or style of another painter, hoping to outdo his rival (and invariably succeeding). If

The artist was so proud of this gorgeous, sun-drenched painting that he wrote in his will exactly where he wanted it to hang in the National Gallery.

27

this behavior seems mean-spirited, it also led Turner to do some of his best work.

Turner seems to have been willing to try anything once, especially if he thought it might spread his name and his work to a larger public. In 1799, amid all his other commissions, we find Turner painting the scenery for a new form of entertainment known as the *eidophusikon,* or panorama. These shows, invented by Philippe Jacques de Loutherbourg in 1781, were the distant forefathers of the movies, although rather than motion pictures, they were pictures in motion. An evening's performance involved several large painted panels that were moved across a stage with dramatic musical accompaniment.

Along with many other artists, Turner was fascinated with de Loutherbourg's sensational new device. Few, however, went so far as to create their own panorama. Motivated both by admiration and by a yearning for fame, Turner painted in 1799 a succession of pictures (now lost) for *The Battle of the Nile,* a panoramic dramatization of an important naval victory in which England's heroic Admiral Nelson vanquished the French fleet, thus maintaining British domination of the seas. Turner's panorama, which was completed just months after the actual battle took place, featured the fiery destruction of a French ship as its climax. Turner was attracted to de Loutherbourg's taste for the sublime, and a suggestion of horror began to creep into his own work. The two spent so much time together that Madame de Loutherbourg eventually accused Turner of "stealing her husband's secrets" and barred him from the house.

Two other events that shaped the course of Turner's life took place in late 1799. First, he was elected an associate of the Royal Academy, which marked his passage from promising student to accepted member of a select community of artists. Next, he moved out of his father's apartments to a studio he shared with another painter. Turner entered the nineteenth century riding on a wave of confidence. In a rare self-portrait from 1798 he presents himself as a young artist to be reckoned with, his dapper attire, fresh face, and frank stare announcing his ambitions loud and clear.

But good fortune was soon replaced by grief. Turner's mother had been subject to violent fits of temper for some time, and in 1800 she was sent off to the Hospital of St. Mary at Bethlehem, where Turner's old patron Dr. Monro cared for her. She was never released. Turner rarely spoke of his mother, but seeing her committed to a lunatic asylum must have affected him profoundly. Exactly how, one can only guess; Turner was a secretive man who kept his private life private. Still, it is worth noting that he never settled down with any one woman, that he lived with his father much of his life, and that he invested so much energy and emotion in his relationship with the Royal Academy.

During the period when Turner belonged to the Royal Academy, landscape was not thought to be a desirable subject for serious artists. Although a country as scenic as Britain was bound to have a rich heritage of landscape painting, only historical, religious, or mythological subjects were considered worthy of highest praise. Around this time, neoclassicism was all the rage in Europe. Early archaeological excavations had captured the public imagination by unearthing the buried remains of ancient cities, and the art, architecture, literature, and civilization of antiquity were studied and held up as ideals.

Painters who wished to stay in step with current taste (or else abandon all hope of selling their pictures) depicted scenes from Greek mythology or the Bible, or they portrayed great military leaders—from ancient or recent history. The art of painting was supposed to enlighten the viewer, to do more than merely delight the senses. How could pretty pictures of the countryside serve these lofty goals? Until 1810, the British Institution (an artists' society that rivaled the R.A.) would not even allow paintings with a landscape background to be entered in its competitions. But Turner saw even greater epic struggles and heroic themes in seascapes and sunsets. Although he was practical enough to begin by working within the accepted boundaries of taste, he was determined to elevate the status of landscape painting one day.

Turner struck his first major blow for the cause with his first historical landscape painting, *The Fifth Plague of Egypt,* exhibited at the R.A. in 1800. Along with the painting's title in the exhibition catalogue was a quotation from the book of Exodus: "The Lord sent thunder and hail and the fire ran along the ground." Although Turner was mistaken about his title—fire was actually the seventh plague—the choice of subject was ideally suited to his purpose of

When he called this painting The Fifth Plague of Egypt, *Turner confused the title of his Biblical catastrophe (fire was the* seventh *plague) but he painted a thrilling landscape nonetheless.*

establishing the power of landscape painting. This biblical theme had been addressed many times before, but most artists placed the figure of Moses at the focal point of the picture. Turner left the humans as tiny details in the foreground, concentrating instead on the furious whirl of smoke and clouds, the wind-whipped trees, the stark pyramid, and the civilization in the distance threatened by the storm. In short, Turner painted the landscape itself, and the result was more awesome than any arrangement of figures could ever be.

All the same, he knew that such an audaciously different picture was a risky undertaking, so he prepared exhaustively. Over a year in advance, he started sketching the apocalyptic scenes of the French master Nicolas Poussin, studying his dynamic compositions and muted, gloomy colors. Turner hoped to capture Poussin's aura of the sublime for his biblical disaster scene, but he also aimed for historical accuracy. His sketchbooks are filled with studies of ancient Egyptian artifacts depicting mythological gods like Osiris, from Egyptian mythology, as well as various archaeological details that can scarcely be detected in the finished work. All of Turner's efforts paid off; the picture was enthusiastically received. Perhaps even more important to Turner was the fact that William Beckford purchased it. Having his own work placed in the same collection as the Claudes he had so admired must have pleased the young artist.

An even greater accomplishment was soon to present itself. Quite without warning, three vacancies appeared among the forty Academicians, the exalted inner circle of the Royal Academy. In February 1802, at the age of twenty-six, Turner found himself elected to fill the first one, becoming the youngest full member of the Royal Academy. His new responsibilities involved politics more than painting, but he plunged into the academic duties with zeal. A year before, Turner would scarcely have dared to dream of becoming a full Academician so soon. Nor could he have realized how much of his education still lay ahead of him.

WHEN TURNER OFFICIALLY JOINED THE ACADEMICIANS OF THE Royal Academy, he felt like a changed man. As one who came from a modest background, the sense of belonging to the inner ranks of an important institution gratified him deeply. He began to change his public image, perhaps in an attempt to live up to his new role. He acquired an extensive library of British poetry and changed his signature from W. Turner to J. M. W. Turner. When the opportunity for exploring the riches of European art came up—thanks to French general and emperor Napoleon Bonaparte—he was ready. It would lead to the next important step in his artistic development.

For most of Turner's life, Britain had been at war. The execution of the

French king and queen in 1793 left all of Europe reeling. After years of turmoil and strife, Napoleon and his mighty army came to power. While he brought temporary stability to France, he raised anew the threat of French aggression. In 1802, however, Britain and France signed the Treaty of Amiens, putting an end to hostilities—until 1803, that is, when war broke out again. For that brief interval, travel to the continent became feasible, opening up a whole new world of possibilities. Turner was among the first to make the pilgrimage, leaving on July 15 for Paris. He knew the crossing would be arduous and the political situation unpredictable. What made Turner risk his life without hesitation? It had always been his nature to seize every new experience and live life to the fullest. More to the point, he knew that Napoleon had assembled all of the spoils from his many military campaigns at the Louvre palace in Paris. The resulting exhibition was a rare opportunity for the artist to feast his eyes on masterpieces from private collections all over Europe. Napoleon's advisor called it "the most astounding collection of art that has ever been formed."

The journey to France was every bit as difficult as Turner might have expected. His ship arrived in a storm, and the longboat he took to shore nearly went down on the way in. Turner memorialized the dramatic scene in drawings, jotting in one sketchbook, "Our landing at Calais; Nearly swampt." Once he and his luggage made it ashore, Turner set off by horse-drawn coach for a journey of ten weeks through the dramatic Swiss Alps—part of a high, rugged mountain range that runs through Switzerland, France, and Italy—and then he headed to Paris. During a period of three months, the artist filled six sketchbooks

The sight of a celebrated sailing ship known as The Fighting Temeraire *being pulled to its final resting place by a steamboat struck Turner as a sign of the changing times. The setting sun highlights the painting's somber mood.*

Turner painted this picture as a memorial to his friend and rival, Sir David Wilkie, who died on board a sailing ship near Gilbraltar and was buried at sea. The artist labored to keep the mast and sail of the boat as mournfully black as possible.

(Pages 39 and 40) The idea for this famous picture began when Turner read about a slave ship on which an epidemic had broken out. The captain ordered the sick slaves thrown overboard because his insurance policy would only pay if they were lost at sea, not if they died of disease.

with more than four hundred sketches as well as copious notes on subjects ranging from the breathtaking scenery to the quality of the wine. He kept returning to his sketchbooks throughout his career, relying on his memory to help him reconstruct on-the-spot notations into a finished painting.

When Turner finally reached the Louvre, he must have been overwhelmed by the rich variety of art spread before him. Though few of the artists were unknown to him, it was his first chance to see their works in person. Besides Poussin, Turner was drawn to Italian painters such as Titian and Raphael, whose bold use of color excited him. He studied their techniques closely, making careful notes on works of particular interest. He drew detailed diagrams of the color arrangements in certain pictures. These notes were only the first sign of Turner's growing preoccupation with pure color.

On returning home, Turner was busier than ever. In 1803, his pictures were selling as fast as he painted them, and he reported having "commissions for twenty years." He continued to exhibit at the Royal Academy, took his dinners at the Academy Club, and sat on the Academy Council. But the young artist with the cockney accent lacked the social and political skills that were a very real part of life at the R.A. Turner seems to have been somewhat full of himself, and he was unable to hold his tongue, which got him into arguments. During one memorable exchange, Turner insulted Sir Francis Bourgeois, landscape painter to the king, who replied by calling Turner "a little reptile." Not to be outdone, Turner told him he was "a great reptile with ill manners."

Turner now was making enough money to convert part of his Harley Street

The artist supposedly had himself lashed to the mast of a ship for several hours during a storm so that he might better understand the effect he was attempting to capture. Nevertheless, the painting was not understood by most critics.

studio into a private gallery. In April 1804, three days after his mother died in the insane asylum, Turner held his first one-man exhibition in his own space. Turner always remained loyal to the Royal Academy, but after a series of arguments in 1805, he temporarily stopped sending pictures to be exhibited and made his own gallery the focus of his efforts.

It was there that he first displayed *The Shipwreck*, one of his most thrilling pictures of adventure at sea, with its seething waters, madly tilting decks, and dark, brooding skies. Much more compelling than *Fishermen at Sea,* his earlier treatment of boats in a storm, *The Shipwreck* is clearly the work of someone who has been in danger on the waves. It later became a very popular engraving, but there is no substitute for seeing the color and texture of the original oil painting.

One of the artist's main innovations was his unorthodox, almost playful technique in applying his paint. "Turner has no settled process," wrote a colleague in 1804, "but drives the colors about till he has expressed the idea in his mind." This freedom of approach caused some critics to refer to his technique as "scribbling" and wonder if he applied paint with a trowel. After seeing a show at Turner's gallery, the artist Benjamin West reported he was "disgusted with what he found there;

(Below and in detail on page 32)

Turner based this dramatic painting, The Shipwreck, *on sketches from actual shipwrecks. It eventually became a popular engraving.*

In 1804, at age twenty-nine, Turner opened a gallery where he exhibited and sold his own work right up until his death. In 1851 his coffin was displayed there so admirers could pay their last respects.

views on the Thames, crude blotches, nothing could be more vicious."

Nonetheless, a few other British artists were beginning to copy Turner's loose, freewheeling style. What was not clear to anyone but Turner was that he had much more radical experiments in mind, ideas so far ahead of their time that they did not make sense to his contemporaries. Having studied the old masters and absorbed what he could from them, he was beginning to break with their rules. Over the next fifty years—and in the face of harsh criticism— Turner would create his own mode of expression.

In the same year Turner exhibited *The Shipwreck*, Britain's Royal Navy was engaged in an important struggle for control of the seas. Admiral Nelson led

H. M. S. *Victory* and the rest of the British fleet against French and Spanish ships at the Battle of Trafalgar. Nelson and his men knew they were the last line of defense against possible invasion by Napoleon. Miraculously, they captured a dozen enemy ships, but Nelson was killed during the fight. When the *Victory* brought his body home, flag flying at half-mast, Turner was standing on shore, sketchbook in hand.

Soon after making sketches of the bittersweet scene, Turner began work on his painting of the historic event. He first exhibited the painting—a complex web of ropes, sails, masts, and smoke—in an unfinished state at his gallery in 1806. It was not completed until two years later, when it became one of the first pictures he showed at the new rival to the Royal Academy, the British Institution.

Turner chose an unusual vantage point for his picture, as if he had been perched up in the ship's rigging as the battle raged on. One effect of this approach was to make the people in the picture seem almost insignificant. One can just barely see Nelson, lying wounded on deck beyond the cluster of red-coated officers in the painting's foreground. Given the amount of detail in the picture, it's hard to believe that Turner was not there to witness the battle himself. But it is entirely a work of memory and imagination. On first seeing Turner's painting, Sir Edwin Landseer, a member of the Royal Academy, called it "the first true epic British picture."

Even as Turner was producing paintings of such originality, lecturers at the Royal Academy were still denigrating his preferred genre—landscape painting—as mere "mapmaking." History painters were still held to be the most important artists. Turner had proven his ability to tackle any genre of painting, but he was painfully aware of the second-class status of his beloved landscape, and he wanted to do something about it. His friend W. E. Wells, a rather undistinguished watercolorist whose worldly savvy Turner respected, had been nag-

Turner's painting was by far the most imaginative interpretation of the Battle of Trafalgar, which was an important British victory in the war against the French, but also a national tragedy due to the death of Admiral Nelson.

ging him to publish a series of prints of his paintings to foil future forgers. After a long pause, Turner replied, "Zounds, gaffer! There will be no peace with you till I begin . . . well, give me a sheet of paper there, rule the size for me, tell me what subject I shall take."

What the two men were talking about eventually took the form of a series of one hundred prints that Turner came to call the *Liber Studorium,* or "book of study." He based the name on Claude Lorrain's *Liber Veritatis,* or "book of truth," which was closer to what Wells had been talking about—a simple record of all the artist's works, intended as a safeguard against forgers. Turner began working on something very different: it was a prolonged investigation of the various types of landscape, intended to educate Turner's public and peers.

Turner carefully listed six varieties of landscape: marine, mountainous, architectural, pastoral, "EP" (by which he probably meant "epic" or "elegant pastoral"), and historical. Some of the sketches he made in preparation for this series are more interesting than the finished prints. He worked on the *Liber Studorium* from 1809 until 1819 but managed to produce only 71 of his proposed 100 prints. Many of these did not sell. All the same, he had made his point. At least where Turner was concerned, people were willing to take landscape more seriously.

Although Turner abandoned his ambitious project, it taught him a great deal about publishing and working with engravers. From that time on, prints

Turner made several sketches on board Admiral Nelson's ship, H.M.S. Victory *shortly before it sailed into battle. He relied on these studies later when he painted his battle scene.*

became an important part of his work and income. Illustrating travel books and volumes of poetry brought Turner's name to a wider public than would ever go to see his paintings at exhibition.

Among other benefits, Turner's increasing notoriety brought him improved opportunities for patronage. This did not mean simply that rich collectors bought his paintings. Art had never been more popular than it was in England during the romantic period. Wealthy patrons welcomed artists to their country estates, where they would be provided with all the inspiration and materials necessary for the creation of art. More often than not, the lord of the manor was an aspiring painter himself, eager for any informal instruction his talented guest might provide.

Turner did his best to take advantage of the gracious offers he received, but, as usual, he sometimes forgot his manners. One such occasion was his visit to the estate of Sir John Fleming Leicester in 1808. Leicester, who had purchased some of the artist's major paintings, invited Turner to come paint two large views of Tabley Hall, his estate in Cheshire. Another artist who was present reports that Turner spent most of his time fishing when he was supposed to be painting. Because the pictures turned out fine, and because Sir John was also an angler, Turner was forgiven. But a journalist named William Jerdan recorded another evening at Tabley Hall that shows what a rude guest Turner could be: "In the drawing room stood a landscape on an easel on which his Lordship was at work as the fancy mood struck him. Of course, when assembled for the tedious half hour before dinner, we all gave our opinions on its progress, its beauties and its defects. I stuck a blue wafer on to show where I thought a bit of bright color or a light would be advantageous; and Turner took the brush and gave a touch, here and there, to mark some improvements." The next morning, Leicester was shocked to receive a bill from Turner for "Instruction in Painting." The artist was not invited back again.

Not all of Turner's relationships with patrons were so strained. In fact, Walter Fawkes of Farnley Hall became Turner's closest friend. Turner visited each year until Fawkes died in 1825. He was more comfortable at Farnley Hall than anywhere else. He played with the children, took part in outdoor activities, and was welcomed not only as a great artist but also as a friend. He kept a studio outfitted there, and the Farnley children were among the only people he allowed to watch him work. Some of the most valued insights into Turner's work habits come from their recollections of time they spent watching him.

One afternoon in 1811, Turner was walking with Fawkes's eldest son, Hawkesworth, when a violent thunderstorm appeared over a nearby valley. Turner produced an envelope from his pocket and began making frantic notes on the back. "He was absorbed," recalled the son. "He was entranced. There was the storm rolling and sweeping and shooting out its lightning over the Yorkshire hills. Presently the storm passed, and he finished. 'There, Hawkey,' said he. 'In two years you will see this again, and call it *Hannibal Crossing the Alps.*'"

Turner's series of prints, the Liber Studorium *was conceived with a grand purpose: to earn greater respect for landscape artists. Though this opening page was quite elaborate, Turner never got around to completing the entire series.*

The picture Turner produced a year later, *Snowstorm: Hannibal and His Army Crossing the Alps,* has become one of his most famous. The memory of the storm in Yorkshire was still fresh in the artist's mind when he painted the huge spiral of wind and snow that dominates the almost eight-foot-long canvas. Turner had

Turner published his work in editions of prints that many people could afford and enjoy. He also collected prints by other artists and enjoyed browsing through them for hours on end.

read about Hannibal, a mighty military leader from ancient Carthage who tried to conquer Rome in 218 B.C. by sending his armies on the backs of elephants across the treacherous Swiss Alps in the dead of winter. In Turner's dark painting, the only signs of the general's forces are a few minuscule soldiers and the tiny curl of an elephant's trunk near the bottom of the picture. The mighty armies are dwarfed by the terrifying power of the storm. Nevertheless, human misconduct continues; in the picture's foreground, thieves or soldiers brutalize a group of helpless travelers. Overhead a pale sun struggles through the storm. Turner fought the Royal Academy Hanging Committee to have his picture lowered so that the sun would be at viewers' eye level.

It is a huge, dark painting that marks a decisive shift in the artist's work toward darker themes. Turner was fond of quoting passages of poetry in exhibition catalogues, and when he showed *Hannibal* he quoted, for the first time, from his own unfinished epic poem with the depressing title "Fallacies of Hope." The painting and its apocalyptic mood may reflect Turner's fears about Napoleon, who had passed through the Alps and was still marching around Europe when the picture was painted. Perhaps the tiny patch of blue sky at the

(Next pages) *Turner planned for eight years before beginning this ambitious painting of Hannibal's army crossing the Alps. The awesome mountain range and whirling snow make the army almost invisible, although a few soldiers and one of the elephants used to pack supplies can be seen near the bottom.*

One of Turner's patrons challenged him to make a picture that would convey the size of a man-of-war sailing ship. He painted this minutely detailed watercolor the same day, entirely from memory.

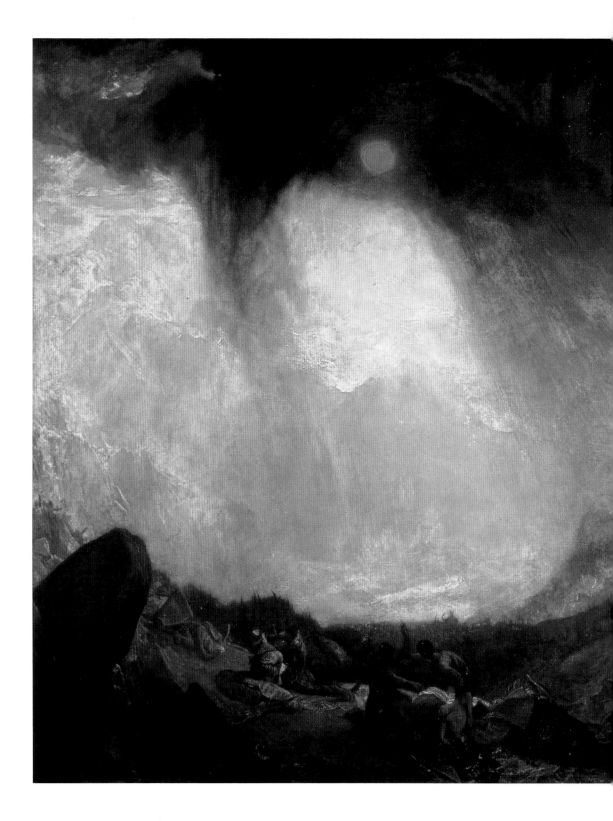

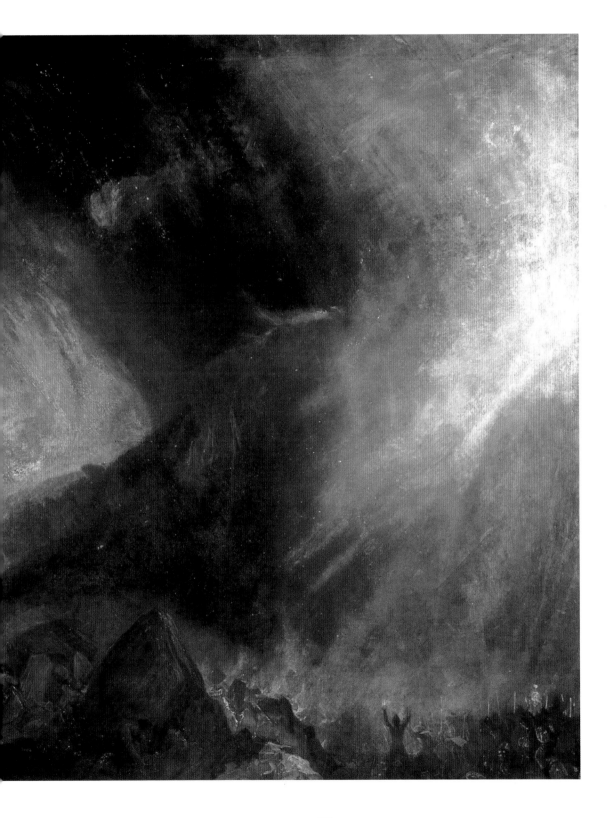

upper left is a sign of hope. Turner himself left theorizing about his art to others. When Lady Eastlake, a friend of the artist, saw the picture in his gallery, she asked, "The end of the world, Mr. Turner?" His reply was: "No, Ma'am. Hannibal crossing the Alps."

It was around this time that he first encountered one of his chief rivals, John Constable. Constable may have envied Turner's success. Both men were landscape painters of about the same age, and though Constable is now remembered with Turner as the other great talent of this period, he was not accepted into the R.A. until after he turned fifty. Constable was a much more precise observer of nature, more botanist than poet. He didn't think much of Turner's free style of painting when, in 1813, the two men chanced to meet. "I dined at the Royal Academy last Monday in the Council Room. . . ." Constable wrote to a friend. "I sat next to Turner, and opposite Mr. West and Lawrence—I was a good deal entertained with Turner. I always expected to find him what I did— he is uncouth but has a wonderful range of mind."

Constable's impression of Turner was more accurate and more profound than he realized. Though Turner never attended formal school, he was a man of wide-ranging interests—from poetry to fishing, archaeology to travel. He could discuss current politics or ancient history; he studied archaeology, called on his old architectural training from time to time, and tried to keep abreast of the latest scientific breakthroughs. All these interests informed his work, sometimes in ways that are not immediately clear on first glance.

An anecdote about Turner at Farnley Hall illustrates his naturally inquisitive approach to his work. At breakfast one morning, Fawkes asked Turner if he thought it possible to make a drawing of ordinary dimensions that would give some idea of the size of a man-of-war, the largest battleship in the British fleet.

"The idea hit Turner's fancy," recalled the niece of Fawkes's son, Hawkesworth, "for with a chuckle he said, 'Come along Hawkey, and we will see what we can do for Papa.' And the boy sat by his side the whole morning and witnessed the evolution of *A First-Rate Taking in Stores*. His description of the way Turner went to work was very extraordinary; he began by pouring wet paint onto the paper till it was saturated. He tore, he scratched, he scrubbed at it in a kind of frenzy and the whole thing was chaos—but gradually and as if by magic, the lovely ship, with all its exquisite minutia, came into being and by luncheon time the drawing was taken down in triumph."

Perhaps the most remarkable thing about this story is the speed with which Turner was able to produce such a complicated watercolor. The fact that Turner met Fawkes's challenge without having to check any visual references is nothing short of amazing. On looking at the finished picture, it's hard to imagine Turner's rough, almost reckless working method, scratching at the surface of the paper with "his eagle claw of a thumbnail."

Turner was always breaking the conventional rules of painting. He used oil-painting techniques in his watercolor pictures and vice versa. He grew fascinated with the paint itself and enjoyed playing with the surface of his pictures in ways that are more common among artists who lived one hundred years later. While most painters employed a soft horsehair or short-bristle paintbrush, Turner sometimes applied great dollops of paint with a flat metal tool known as a palette knife. Turner tried every kind of paint and glaze he could get his hands on, combining them in unorthodox ways to suit his needs.

Turner's relentless desire to experiment drove him to creative heights, but it also opened him up to fierce critical attack. His rival John Constable derided Turner's more fanciful paintings as "airy visions painted with tinted steam." A prominent critic dismissed the work as "pictures of nothing and the very like." Today, when abstract painting is accepted, the critic's attack rings true: his insult has ripened into an insight.

Chapter Four

"You mayn't believe it!"

TURNER WAS FORTY YEARS OLD IN 1815, WHEN NAPOLEON was defeated at the Battle of Waterloo after one final attempt to seize power. The former French emperor was exiled for good, leaving Europe relatively peaceful and rekindling Turner's thoughts of travel to the continent. Though he was by this time a veteran tourist, Turner had never been to Italy, the land revered as the birthplace of the art of painting. Many of the masters Turner admired had lived and worked in Italy, and his style had been indirectly shaped by this place he had never visited. "Turner should come to Rome," wrote Sir Thomas Lawrence to a fellow member of the Royal Academy. "The subtle harmony of the atmosphere, that wraps everything

in its own milky sweetness . . . can only be rendered, according to my belief, by the beauty of his tones."

Turner would have left right away if he could have, but it was four years before he finally set off on his pilgrimage to Italy. One reason for the delay may have been that he was considering marrying a woman named Clara Wells, the daughter of his artist friend, W. F. Wells. (He had lost touch with Sarah Danby and her children.) But he did not marry Clara, who later wrote that "He was a

The thirsty dog at the edge of the water establishes the mood of this warm sunset scene and shows Turner's sharp eye for details. (See the enlargement on the previous page.)

firm, affectionate friend to the end of his life. No one could have imagined under that rather rough and cold exterior, how strong were the affections which lay hidden beneath." Turner continued to live with his father and spent his Christmases with the Fawkes family at Farnley Hall.

To prepare for the trip to Italy, Turner consulted the popular guidebooks, making lists of the places he wanted to see. He brushed up on the Italian language and compiled notebooks full of helpful hints on everything from purifying water to obtaining a passport. But by 1817 his work load was so demanding that he could not get away. As a consolation prize, he traveled to Belgium and Holland and toured along the Rhine River. On his return, as if to compound his longing, James Hakewill commissioned Turner to illustrate a book entitled *Picturesque Tour of Italy,* based on the author's sketches. At that time there was almost a set itinerary for young gentlemen on their "grand tour" of Europe, and Turner became familiar with many sights before he even set foot in Italy.

What he could not have been prepared for, when he finally made the trip in August 1819, was the quality of Italian light. Although his work did not change overnight, there is little doubt that Turner's first glimpse of a golden sunset over the Mediterranean Sea forever altered the course of his art. More than anything he saw in the galleries of Venice, more than any views he sketched, it was this light—so different from the cold sunshine of England—that made possible the radical experiments with pure color that were to occupy him later.

Turner made all the obligatory stops on that first journey. He traveled briskly, sketched furiously, and preferred not to linger in any place for very long. After a brief stay in Venice, he spent the longest time in Rome. Turner was seen sketching all over town; he made some 1,500 pencil sketches during those two months in Rome.

While he was in Rome, the nearby volcano Mount Vesuvius erupted, as it had in A.D. 79, when it buried the Roman port city of Pompeii under tons of ash and hot lava. The city had been discovered by archaeologists twenty years before Turner's birth, and since the artist was also interested in archaeology, he would surely have been thrilled at the chance to witness one of history's great natural disasters repeat itself. He made the trip to Naples, but this time Vesuvius's wrath was far less cataclysmic. Instead of running for their lives, Turner and an architect friend climbed the mountain, and later that evening he dined with the British Ambassador to Italy.

After spending Christmas in Florence, Turner decided to return home through the Swiss Alps in the middle of winter—repeating Hannibal's mistake, with only slightly less disastrous results. The mountain pass through which he had entered months before was now blocked by snow, so Turner took his rented coach over Mont Cenis. Not surprisingly, the carriage capsized at the top. Turner narrated the rest of the adventure in a letter to a friend: "The carriage door [was] so completely frozen that we were obliged to get out at the window—the guide and Cantonier began to fight, and the driver was by a process verbal put into prison . . . we had to march or rather flounder up to our knees nothing less in snow all the way down."

Turner didn't let such hardships get in the way of a good picture. To judge by the notes in one of his sketchbooks ("men shoveling away snow for the carriage—Women and children hugging—the sky pink—the light and the cast shadows rather warm—Trees are all covered with the snow"), Turner seems to have continued sketching throughout the mishap. This may not have made him very popular with his traveling companions (especially the ones who had to shovel the snow), but on his return he presented Fawkes with a lovely watercolor of his adventure at Mont Cenis pass.

After his Italian experiences, Turner must have been anxious to put all he had seen and learned into his art. In 1820, he exhibited a picture that reflects this

Based on a subject from Roman mythology, this idyllic painting even won praise from Turner's most critical rivals.

desire. Though it was strongly criticized at the Royal Academy, the painting, with its long descriptive title, *Rome, from the Vatican. Raffaelle, Accompanied by La Fornarina Preparing His Pictures for the Decoration of the Loggia* is interesting for what it says about Turner's state of mind. In a surprisingly unrealistic scene, paintings from the Vatican collection are strewn around an outdoor terrace as Raphael, the Italian master Turner most admired, ponders his paintings, while his mistress, a woman known as La Fornarina, gazes into the distance. Behind the couple extends a sweeping view of the city. The terrace is flanked by vast corridors that open to the left and right, suggesting spaces within spaces, and more rooms full of riches. Turner here confronts the amount of great art he has seen during his trip, and he also captures the Italian love of surface ornament. But it is easy to see that when he painted this picture he had not yet begun to make sense of the Italian light. This would take more time.

In the meantime, Turner opened a new gallery. He had spent years building it, but the turnout for the first exhibition in 1822 was disappointing. The following year, Turner was commissioned by George IV, the King of England, to paint a new, larger picture of the Battle of Trafalgar. He earned his highest fee yet, six hundred guineas, and poured his heart into the gigantic painting, only to be insulted by the seamen at the Court of Saint James, where the picture was to be hung. They insisted that Turner revise the painting in the interest of "historical accuracy," because Turner had condensed several dramatic events of the battle into one scene. He grudgingly consented, but when the picture was finally rejected and sent to a gallery in Greenwich, Turner was deeply offended.

One high point of 1823 was the exhibition of a very different sort of pic-

This enormous view of Rome reflects Turner's excitement after visiting Italy for the first time. Deeply impressed by the works of the Italian masters, he included the great artist Raphael in his painting.

ture, based on a subject from Roman mythology: *The Bay of Baiae, with Apollo and the Sibyl*. Even Constable had to pay respect to this glowing idyllic landscape. "Turner is stark mad with ability," he wrote. "The picture seems painted with saffron and indigo." This was by no means Turner's ultimate expression of the effects of Italian light, but something was definitely beginning to change in the atmosphere of his landscapes.

During one of his lectures at the Royal Academy, Turner spoke highly of the Dutch master Rembrandt, an artist he had previously disparaged. Turner seems to have changed his mind about Rembrandt, rhapsodizing about "that matchless veil of color, that lucid interval of morning dawn and dewey light on which the eye dwells so completely enthralled." Though Turner had sometimes complained about the sloppiness of Rembrandt's forms, now he called it a "sacrilege to pierce the mystic shell of color in search of form." This statement is not just a minor shift in the artist's taste; it represents a breakthrough in approach that Turner would pursue in his own work for the rest of his days.

Around this point in Turner's career, he began to produce unfinished works on paper that are now known as his "color beginnings." Although the artist saved these simple compositions of pure color, it is unlikely that he ever intended them to be exhibited. They may have been studies for other works, or a method of organizing the color tones in a picture, but since they resemble the abstract works of the twentieth century, they have been celebrated by several generations of artists after Turner's death.

These "color beginnings" indicate that Turner was thinking about light and color as suitable subjects for art in themselves, independent from any recognizable subject. Even the more conventional paintings Turner exhibited during the next few years, such as the gorgeous harbour scene *Cologne, the Arrival of a Packet Boat, Evening* (1826) and *Mortlake Terrace, the Seat of William Moffatt, Esq., Summer's Evening* (1827), show a marked change in his handling of light and

Turner would try anything to improve a composition. The black dog in this picture was cut out and pasted on the canvas after the painting was finished.

color. The latter picture is especially radical: the artist has set up his easel facing into the sunset, which casts heavy shadows across the picture and nearly blinds the viewer. Rays from the burning sun drown out the other elements of the picture: boats racing on the Thames River below, the woman and child strolling on the grass, even the black dog in the center of the picture (which Turner playfully cut out of a sketchbook and stuck on the canvas).

British critics made fun of the unusual effect. "He is in painting what a cook would be in gastronomy," wrote one reviewer. "Fancying he could make a good curry, [he] curried everything he could get hold of, fish, meat, fowl, and vegetables: MR. TURNER, indeed, goes further, for he curries the rivers, and the bridges, and the boats upon the river, and the ladies and gentlemen in the boats." But twenty years later, a Frenchman named Théophile Thoré wrote that this same work "represents for me the genius of Turner in all its extraordinary freedom, completely independent of any influence from the old masters. . . . There is too much sunlight, dispersed through the misty and dusty atmosphere, for us to be able to see clearly what is round about. All that we can see of trees and stonework is enveloped in, and devoured by the light; everything seems to be made of light itself, and even to emit rays and flashes of light."

John Ruskin, seen here in a self-portrait, devoted most of his life to writing about Turner's art and defending his genius against angry critics, but the artist himself resisted Ruskin's lofty praise.

Though Turner continued to produce more conventional work calculated to suit the public taste—such as his enormously popular illustrations for the book *Italy* by Samuel Rogers—the work that mattered most to him was more experimental. He seemed to be steadily losing patience with conventional tastes. To a woman who questioned his use of color, he asked, "Don't you see that yourself in nature? Because, if you don't, heaven help you." Of the strange hues in an 1826 watercolor, *Red Sunset on a Hill Fortress,* the critic John Ruskin later wrote: "Such things *are,* though you mayn't believe it!"

In 1829, Turner resolved to travel once more to Italy, and this time to stay long enough to actually work in the magical Mediterranean sunlight. He asked a colleague in Italy to prepare a workable studio for him, specifying "plenty of the useful, but nothing of the ornamental." After two months in Rome, he exhibited three of the pictures he had been working on, and the show was attacked by the Italian critics. Turner spent the rest of his time in Rome studying Michelangelo's frescoes on the Sistine Chapel ceiling, and he continued his tireless sketching until it was time to depart.

"I have fortunately met up with a good-tempered, funny, little, elderly man, who will probably be my traveling companion throughout the journey," wrote another traveler leaving Italy. "He is continually popping his head out of the window to sketch whatever strikes his fancy, and became quite angry because the conductor would not wait for him whilst he took a sunrise view of Macareta. 'Damn the fellow!' says he, 'He has no feeling.' He speaks but a few words of Italian, about as much French, which two languages he jumbles together most amusingly. His good temper, however, carries him through all trouble. I am sure you would love him for his indefatigability in his favorite pursuit. From his conversation he is evidently *near kin to* if not absolutely, an artist. Probably you may know of him. The name on the trunk is, J.W. or J. M.W. Turner!"

Once again, as Turner's coach attempted to cross Mont Cenis, it tipped over in the snow. It was the last time he would make this crossing for another twelve years. He had hoped to return the following year, and had even left his Italian studio intact, but his plans were to change. Back in London, Turner exhibited an outstanding new painting on a subject that he had first sketched twenty years before, *Ulysses Deriding Polyphemus.* In a scene from Homer's ancient epic poem *The Odyssey,* Ulysses, the heroic warrior, and his men sail away after escaping from the clutches of a Cyclops—a giant, man-eating monster with one eye— known as Polyphemus. Turner used his first-hand experience of Mount

Vesuvius in rendering the Cyclops's volcano home, and the picture features one of the artist's most beautiful sunsets. Nevertheless, it did not find a buyer.

Three months later, on September 21, 1829, Turner's father died at the age of eighty-five. While the death cannot be called unexpected, it was still a terrible shock to the artist. He said he "felt like he had lost an only child." Turner was always much closer to his father than to anyone else in his life. For many years after he became a famous artist, his father had helped manage Turner's business affairs and even served as a painter's assistant, stretching canvases and mixing colors. The death of his parent forced him to confront his own mortality, and

Ruskin was a passionate collector of Turner prints and watercolors, which hung on the walls surrounding his bed.

Turner began thinking more and more about the legacy he wanted to leave behind.

Just nine days after his father's funeral, Turner drew up his first will. Although his material wealth was by this time considerable, his will placed more emphasis on artistic concerns. It provided for a professorship of landscape painting at the Royal Academy, or else a biannual medal to be called the Turner Prize, to be awarded to the best landscape painting of the year. He also set aside money to establish "almshouses for decayed English artists (landscape painters only) and single men."

Another condition of the unusual will was that England's National Gallery

This extravagantly colorful scene was inspired by a passage from Homer's epic poem, The Odyssey, *in which Ulysses, the hero, escapes from a huge one-eyed monster called Polyphemus.*

should receive two of his early historical landscapes, *Dido Building Carthage* (1815)—which he considered one of his very best paintings—and *Decline of the Carthaginian Empire* (1817), "to hang between two Claudes." Concerned that all his best work should remain together, Turner began using his wealth to buy back paintings from private collections. He also purchased the work of other artists he admired, and sometimes other relics as well. He bought Sir Joshua Reynolds's palette, and in 1831 he purchased a plaster cast taken from the skull of Raphael, a creepy curio that attests to Turner's continued fascination with the Italian master.

That same year, Turner made drawings for Sir Walter Scott's *Collected Poems.* The poet and the painter argued about money, but deep down they respected each other's work. "Turner's palm is itchy as his fingers are ingenious," wrote Scott to a friend. "He will, take my word for it, do nothing without cash and anything for it." Scott's remarks are only a slight exaggeration. By this point in his career, Turner was acutely aware of the differences between the work he did for money and the work he found personally rewarding. Though his book illustrations allowed him to develop certain themes that recurred in his more serious work, Turner did them mostly "for cash."

After the death of his father, coming just four years after the death of his dear friend and patron Walter Fawkes, one of Turner's few pleasures were his trips to Petworth Hall, the country estate of the third earl of Egremont. Lord Egremont maintained a sort of artist's retreat at his sumptuously furnished estate. Turner made a series of informal interior sketches of Petworth, many of which show musical instruments, Oriental vases, draped statues, and other decorative objects cluttering the floor. These works are unusually intimate and personal for Turner, who even made a painting of himself at work. He seems to have been charmed by the friendly ambience and the company of other artists.

The passing years did not dull Turner's competitive nature. To make his

Turner thought that Dido Building Carthage *was the best of all his works. The conflict between ancient Carthage and Rome held the artist's interest for years and he based several pictures on the subject.*

Royal Academy exhibitions of the 1830s more interesting, he enjoyed the challenge of completing his pictures at the last minute, during what were known as "varnishing days." These last three days before an exhibition were set aside for artists to hang their new works and apply a coat of varnish, a clear liquid that hardened to give oil paintings a protective and lustrous finish. Turner became legendary for showing up at the R.A. with unfinished pictures and completing them before either hanging them or varnishing them as his astonished colleagues looked on. He took great pleasure in doing what he knew no other artist could do so quickly. But he was not just showing off; the eleventh-hour finishes allowed him to size up the work of his rivals and outdo it.

To the summer exhibition of 1832, Turner's old nemesis Constable brought a brightly colored canvas entitled *Whitehall Stairs, or the Opening of the Waterloo Bridge.* As the artist C. R. Leslie tells it, Turner had come with "a grey picture, beautiful and true, but with no positive color in any part of it. Constable's *Waterloo* seemed as if painted with liquid gold and silver, and Turner came several times into the room. . . . Turner stood behind him looking from the *Waterloo* to his own picture, and at last brought his palette from the great room

With this painting, Turner included the following caption: "Rome [was] determined on the overthrow of her hated rival....The Carthaginians, in their anxiety for peace, consented to give up even their arms and their children." The red-tinged clouds overhead suggest the destruction of Carthage.

where he was touching another picture, and putting a round daub of red lead, somewhat bigger than a shilling, on his grey sea, went away without saying a word. The intensity of the red lead, made more vivid by the coolness of his picture, caused even the vermilion and the lake of Constable to look weak. I came into the room just as Turner left it. 'He has been here,' said Constable, 'and fired a gun.' "

Constable's remark reveals how much the two artists were aware of their

competition with each other. Turner's sense of drama was so exaggerated as to seem almost comical. Leslie continued: "The great man did not come again into the room for a day and a half; and then, in the last moments that were allowed for painting, he glazed the scarlet seal he had put on his picture, and shaped it into a buoy."

In 1834, another of the fixtures in Turner's life disappeared. The historic Houses of Parliament, seat of Great Britain's government, which had stood across the Thames for as long as Turner could remember, were destroyed by fire. It was a sensational event, which drew hundreds of spectators. One newspaper account said that some onlookers were "so struck with the grandeur of the sight that they involuntarily . . . clapped their hands, as though they had been present at the closing scene of some dramatic spectacle."

Turner and a few other artists observed the scene from a boat, sketching well into morning. He was captivated by the brilliant flames rising into the night sky and reflecting off the surface of the water. Turner's watercolors were made so

The sketch opposite is one of the few pictures in which Turner pictured himself at work. The scene is Petworth Hall, the country estate of one of Turner's wealthiest patrons. Above is a modern photograph of Petworth.

rapidly that the pages of his sketchbook stuck together.

Less than four months later, Turner exhibited at the British Institution two full-scale oil paintings of the conflagration. Here at last was a subject that seemed to demand Turner's dramatic colors and exuberant brushwork. Once again, he did most of the real painting during the varnishing day, resulting in one of the most detailed descriptions of the eccentric master showing off.

"Turner was there and at work before I came," wrote E. V. Rippingille, the painter who witnessed and recorded the spectacle, "having set-to at the earliest hour allowed. Indeed it was quite necessary to make the best of his time, as the picture when sent in was a mere dab of several colors, and 'without form and void' like the chaos before the creation. . . . for the three hours I was there—and I understood it had been the same since he began in the morning—he never ceased to work, or even once looked or turned from the wall on which his picture was hung. . . .

"A small box of colors, a few very small brushes, and a vial or two were at

When the Houses of Parliament burned to the ground in 1834, Turner joined a huge crowd on the banks of the Thames River and frantically sketched the disaster. This is one of three finished paintings he made of that night.

his feet, very inconveniently placed; but his short figure, stooping, enabled him to reach what he wanted very readily. Leaning forward and sideways over to the right, the left-hand metal button of his blue coat rose six inches higher than the right, and his head buried in his shoulders and held down, presented an aspect curious to all beholders, who whispered their remarks to each other, and quietly laughed to themselves. . . .

"Presently the work was finished: Turner gathered his tools together, put them into and shut up the box, and then, with his face still turned to the wall, and at the same distance from it, went sidling off, without speaking a word to anybody, and when he came to the staircase, in the center of the room, hurried down as fast as he could. All looked with a half-wondering smile, and Maclise, who stood near, remarked, 'There, that's masterly, he does not stop to look at his work; he *knows* it is done, and he is off.'"

The narrator's attention to every detail of Turner's grand performance indicates his respect for the master. But the paintings he produced that day proved too lurid for prevailing taste and did not sell.

Turner had become an obvious target for the amusement of art critics. He was eccentric and successful, and his pictures were becoming more and more unlike the kind of conventional paintings most people were used to seeing. "Splendid combinations of color," wrote one critic, "but they are destitute of all appearance of solidity. Every object appears transparent and soft. They look as though they were made of confectionary's Sugar Candy Jellies." Turner was sometimes hurt by these remarks, but he occasionally showed a sense of humor about it all. Once, at dinner with friends, he jokingly analyzed the salad in terms of his painting. On another occasion, when he heard that a patron had expressed disappointment because the picture he had commissioned had turned out so "indistinct," Turner replied, "You should tell him indistinctness is my forte."

Chapter Five

A Modern Painter

THE SPORT OF POKING FUN AT TURNER REACHED A LOW POINT

in the early 1840s with this skit performed in a Christmas pantomime, as

recalled by Sir Wyke Bayliss, president of the Royal Academy: "Scene: a

picture-dealer's shop on the street. In the window is a painting by J. M. W.

Turner, crimson and gold and white, at which a crowd are gazing with

blind eyes and open mouths. Amongst the crowd is a baker's lad with a

square tray of confectionary on his head. Elbowed by the crowd, he loses

his balance, and the tray falls, smashing the window and plunging through

the wonderful canvas."

Once the picture dealer gets over his state of horror, he realizes that the baker's tray fits perfectly into the picture frame, and that it is daubed all over with crimson and gold from the jam tarts it was carrying. A bag of finely-ground flour is also among the wreckage. "He scatters a little of the flour over the jam tarts and the harmony is complete—crimson and gold and white. The tray is fixed into the picture frame, and ten minutes later an old gentleman, a well-known connoisseur, walks leisurely down the street. He sees the new

The subject of this painting is a citizen of ancient Carthage named Regulus, whose punishment for treason was to have his eyelids cut off and be blinded by the sun. Curiously, Regulus does not seem to appear anywhere; it has been suggested that Turner painted the picture from Regulus's point of view with the bright sun shining in his face.

Turner, buys it at once for a thousand pounds and—all's well that ends well."

Meanwhile, Turner's close friends were rapidly disappearing. In 1837, both Constable and Lord Egremont died. Without Constable, Turner had no rival to motivate him (though Sir Augustus Callcott, a longtime follower of Turner's, had been knighted by Queen Victoria that same year). After Egremont's death,

Turner never went to Petworth again, except on the occasion of the funeral, which he later attempted to paint but could not ever bring himself to complete.

The next three years brought three of Turner's most somber pictures—all of them sea pieces. *The "Fighting Temeraire" Tugged to Her Last Berth to Be Broken Up* depicts a gallant British sailing ship—which had helped win the Battle of Trafalgar—towed by a small, black steamboat, belching smoke, to its final resting place. Although based on an actual event, Turner's painting, as usual, transcends its basic subject

This detail from Slavers Throwing Overboard the Dead and Dying— Typhoon Coming On *(shown in full on pages 39–40) focuses on the human tragedy of the event.*

matter to make a larger point. With the setting sun to the right and the rising moon to the left, the work becomes a meditation on time itself, implying that the birth of the modern era must mean the death of another one.

In 1840 Turner produced a far less romantic vision of ships at sea, *Slavers Throwing Overboard the Dead and Dying—Typhoon Coming On*. Slavery had been abolished in England since 1833, but the horrors of the slave trade were still

emerging. Turner had read about a ship whose human cargo had been perish-
ing of some contagious disease. The captain knew he could collect insurance if
the slaves were lost at sea, but not if they died from ill health, so he ordered
them thrown overboard. Turner's picture leaves little doubt on his own feelings
about slavery. The red sunlight reflected on the water in Turner's picture blends
with the blood of the innocents being devoured by sharks, while the gathering
storm carries the suggestion—if not the promise—of divine retribution.

The following year, Turner lost yet another friend when the artist David

"Some little vessel has gone down in the night," wrote Ruskin of this melancholy watercolor, "all hands lost. A single dog has come ashore. Utterly exhausted, its limbs failing under it, and sinking into the sand, it stands howling and shivering." (A detail from this work, called Dawn After the Wreck, *is shown on page 78.)*

Wilkie died at sea while returning from the Near East. Turner told another artist working on a painting of Wilkie's burial as seen from the ship's deck, "I will do it as it must have appeared off the coast." *Peace—Burial at Sea* is one of the most moving pictures Turner ever painted. It reflects the artist's general state of mind at the time as well as his grief over the passing of his friend. The brilliant torches from the burial party are the only source of light on the very quiet, very dark ship. When a colleague told him that the ship's sails were too black, Turner replied, "I only wish I had any color to make them blacker." The use of rich black tones had been one of Wilkie's specialties. It has been suggested that the tiny black duck flying along the water's surface in the foreground of the picture is a last touch of good-humored rivalry between Turner and his lost friend. Mallord was one of J. M. W. Turner's names, and his friends sometimes jokingly called him a mallard duck.

Just how Turner was weathering all this bad news can be gathered from this description of him by the artist Richard Redgrave: "In person Turner had little of the outward appearance that we love to attribute to the possessors of genius. In the last twenty years of his life, during which we knew him well, his short figure had become corpulent—his face, perhaps from continual exposure to the air, was unusually red, and a little inclined to blotches. . . . He generally

83

wore what is called a black dress-coat, which would have been the better for brushing—the sleeves were mostly too long, coming down over his fat and not over-clean hands. . . . This, together with his ruddy face, his rollicking eye, and his continuous, although, except to himself, unintelligible jokes, gave him the appearance of one of that now wholly extinct race—a long-stage coachman."

Turner must have seemed like a refugee from another time when he was introduced to his young admirer John Ruskin, who went on to become his staunchest supporter and England's most famous art critic. "Everybody has described him to me as boorish, unintellectual, vulgar," Ruskin wrote in his diary. "This I knew to be impossible. I found in him a somewhat eccentric, keen-mannered, matter-of-fact, English-minded gentleman: good-natured evidently, bad-tempered evidently, hating humbug of all sorts, shrewd, perhaps a little selfish, highly intellectual, the powers of his mind not brought out with any delight in their manifestation, or intention of display, but flashing out occasionally in a word or a look."

Ruskin counted this meeting in 1840 as a "principal event in my life," but for his part, Turner seemed unimpressed and perhaps a little put off. Ruskin's boundless enthusiasm for Turner's art—which would help defend the artist's reputation after his death—was rather annoying in person. "I must have talked some folly," Ruskin reasoned after their chilly encounter. "There were few things he hated more than hearing people gush about particular drawings. He knew it merely meant that they could not see the others."

But public taste was shifting, and Turner would need a defender as he continued to push the boundaries of what could be captured in paint. In 1842 he exhibited a remarkable picture, entitled *Snowstorm—Steam-boat Off a Harbour's Mouth Making Signals in Shallow Water, and Going By the Lead*. At first glance, it is difficult to see the boat at all, but it is there, somewhere behind the swirling sheets of snow, wind, and waves. The lack of clear visibility is exactly the point of the picture; "going by the lead" meant that the boat's captain could not see where he was going and had to proceed slowly with a lead weight on the end of a rope to measure the water's depth and keep him from running aground. Turner gave the picture this caption: "The author was in this storm on the night the *Ariel* left Harwich."

As might be expected, the picture suffered harsh criticism. One critic called it "soap suds and whitewash." Turner was even more annoyed when a sympathetic acquaintance told him that his mother had been through such a storm and "understood what he was getting at." The artist replied sharply, "I did not paint it to be understood, but I wished to show what such a scene was like: I got the sailors to lash me to the mast to observe it. I was lashed for four hours, and I did not expect to escape, but I felt duty-bound to record it if I did." It seems unlikely that Turner could have survived such an experience at his age, but the picture is convincing enough whether he was really lashed to the mast or not.

The following year, Ruskin published the first volume of his lengthy defense of Turner, entitled *Modern Painters*. His central premise was that Turner was the first artist to depict nature accurately in all its truth. Ruskin argued convincingly that by recording the fleeting effects of light, weather, and atmosphere, Turner showed what the snowstorm—or the sunset, or the railway—was really like, even though his paintings looked strange next to conventional versions of these phenomena.

Ironically, although no one did more to secure Turner's lasting reputation than Ruskin, the artist himself was anything but appreciative of Ruskin's work. "He sees more in my pictures than I ever painted," said the artist on inspecting a volume of *Modern Painters*. It also bothered Turner that Ruskin's favorite method of praise was to insult the work of other artists, many of whom Turner admired.

Nonetheless, Ruskin watched over and defended the artistic legacy that Turner was so concerned with preserving. As time passed Turner made numerous additions to his will, specifying first that all his paintings remain together, and later the sketches and watercolors as well. He knew where he wanted certain pictures to hang, and in the last rewrite of his will, he specified that he wanted to be buried in Saint Paul's cathedral, near the tombs of Sir Joshua Reynolds and Sir Thomas Lawrence, "among my brothers in art."

Aside from the details of his burial, many of Turner's requests were ignored. Ruskin, who was put in charge of cataloging Turner's vast body of work, destroyed many drawings of a sexual nature because he thought them "unworthy" of Turner (or was offended by their content). Turner wanted all of his pictures—350 oil paintings and more than 20,000 watercolors and drawings—to be exhibited together in a special gallery, a request that was fulfilled only a few years ago with the opening of a special addition to the Tate Gallery in London. Turner also disinherited all his relatives, leaving his sizable fortune to establish his fund for down-and-out landscape painters. His relatives were outraged and contested the will in court. The final outcome was that the nation got the pictures, the family got the money, and Turner's fund for artists was forgotten.

While riding on the brand new train of England's Great Western Railway, Turner stuck his head out the window and even convinced his fellow travelers to do likewise.

Artists never forgot Turner. The famous French Impressionist movement drew heavily on Turner's rendering of light and atmosphere. Two of these French artists, Claude Monet and Camille Pissarro, visited London in 1870 and were deeply impressed with a show of Turner works there. An etching of one of Turner's later pictures, *Rain, Steam, and Speed—the Great Western Railway,* was

even included in the first Impressionist exhibition in Paris. Monet, however, downplayed Turner's influence. "Formerly I liked Turner very much," he said, "today I like him much less—why?—he didn't organize the color enough and he used too much of it." But Monet admitted, "I studied him well."

Another modern French artist, Paul Signac, said that "the works of Turner proved to me that we must be free of all ideas of imitation and copying, and that hues must be created." Henri Matisse traveled to London in 1898 for the express purpose of seeing the Turners. Many years later, Matisse wrote (inaccu-

Turner first painted this picture in 1807, but when he saw it again in 1849, he was dissatisfied and insisted on reworking it extensively for a period of six days. It became one of the last oil paintings he ever exhibited.

rately but affectionately), "Turner lived in a cellar. Once a week he threw open the shutters, and then, what incandescences! What dazzle! What jewelry!"

With the passage of time, Turner's art has come to be generally appreciated and has influenced more generations of artists. As late as 1948, an exhibition of Turner's late works at a contemporary art fair caused a sensation among abstract artists. And an unfinished Turner was purchased not so many years ago for what was then the highest price ever paid for any picture.

Was he a romantic? A modern? A genius? These questions begin to lose importance after a while. "The impression [Turner] made on me was just that of . . . great *general* ability and quickness," said one acquaintance after his death. "Whatever subject of talk was started, he seemed master of it—books, politics, &c. This confirms me in my general view of art—that it is less the product of a special faculty than of a powerful or genial nature, expressing itself through paint or marble." Perhaps it is better to remember him as a man who loved life, lived to make art, and never tired of watching the sun over the water.

In his last days, he moved to a small cottage near the Thames. A visitor in 1851 recalls him in the upstairs room: "and there he would be often at daybreak watching the scenery of the river. The upper or western view he called the English view, and that down the river the Dutch view. During his last illness the weather was dull and cloudy, and he often said in a restless way, 'I should like to see the sun again.'

"Just before his death he was found prostrate on the floor, having tried to creep to the window, but in his feeble state he had fallen in the attempt. It was pleasing to be told that at last the sun broke through the cloudy curtain which so long had obscured its splendour, and filled the chamber of death with the glory of light."

And if it's worth believing that some lives do have perfect endings, his last words were supposed to have been: "The sun is God."

List of Illustrations

Index